Flying SOLO

how to soar above your lonely feelings,
make friends, and find the happiest you

Flying SOLO

how to soar above your lonely feelings, make friends, and find the happiest you

by Pascale Perrier
illustrated by Klaas Verplancke
edited by Erin Zimring

sunscreen

Library of Congress Cataloging-in-Publication Data:
Perrier, Pascale.
[Vous vous sentez seul. English]
Flying Solo / by Pascale Perrier with Erin Zimring ;
illustrated by Klaas Verplancke.
p. cm.—(Sunscreen)
ISBN-13: 978-0-8109-9281-8
ISBN-10: 0-8109-9281-7
1. Loneliness in adolescence. 2. Friendship in adolescence. 3.
Solitude. I. Zimring, Erin. II. Title.
BF724.3.L64P4713 2007
158.2'50835—dc22
2006023609

Translated by Graham Robert Edwards

Book series design by Higashi Glaser Design
Production manager: Alexis Mentor

Printed and bound in China
10 9 8 7 6 5 4 3 2 1

HNA ■■■■■
harry n. abrams, inc.
a subsidiary of La Martinière Groupe
115 West 18th Street
New York, NY 10011
www.hnabooks.com

contents

Phase 2: HOW TO STOP FEELING LONELY

Phase 3: FINDING SOLITUDE

WHY DO I FEEL SO LONELY? I WISH I HAD MORE FRIENDS. NOBODY UNDERSTANDS ME. HOW CAN I BE LESS ISOLATED? I'M TIRED OF BEING ALONE.

At every stage of life, there are times when we feel alone. Babies cry when their mothers leave them. Children feel isolated when their friends and family aren't around.

Most adults look for someone to spend their lives with. But what about when you're a teenager? Adolescence is a time when the physical and psychological changes—which are caused by puberty—make you experience a different type of loneliness. It's a transitional period where just being yourself sometimes feels very uncomfortable. There are new things to worry about, and they affect how you behave. Suddenly, you have a tendency to feel sad and alone; you get lost in your thoughts and problems. This is all totally normal—after all, it takes time to adjust to the person you're becoming! No doubt, it's a bumpy ride from childhood to adulthood. And the feelings of isolation that wash over you from time to time seem to come with the question: "Why do I feel so different from everybody else?"

You may wonder how long those kinds of feelings are going to last, and what you can do about them. That's what this little book is about—the lonely feelings that come with being a teenager. They may come occasionally, or you may have them all the time. But no matter what, you can understand what they're about and successfully deal with them.

NOBODY LOVES ME!

WHY DO I FEEL ALONE?

turning

inward

shyness

are you judging me?

the need for affection

feeling
lonely?

Most people think that being all by yourself and feeling isolated go together. It seems logical that you'd feel alone only when you are separated from others, that as long as you're around friends or family, you won't feel lonely, right? Not really! Adolescence is a time when you can feel very alone, even in a crowd. The explanation is simple: When you're a teenager or preteen, everything gets stirred up. Things you used to be sure of don't seem so certain anymore; your ideas change. *You* change. And you don't know how you fit in with the people around you.

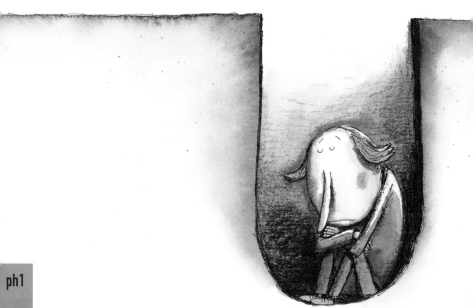

You're afraid to tell others what you're feeling. Lots of times it's like their lives are miles away from yours. And when you feel different from everyone around you, it's lonely.

As far as your family goes, maybe you're not sure how to show affection to your parents anymore. When you were younger you used to give them hugs and kisses, but now the idea of that seems weird and awkward. You still love them, but you don't know how to express it, and it makes your relationship with them different somehow. It's weird, because even when you're in the same house as your parents you can still feel alone.

Sometimes the lonely feeling washes over you during the day for a few minutes—maybe when you're waiting with friends for the school bus, or when you're at your locker getting a notebook. But those moments can stick to you all day like gum on your shoe. Sometimes it feels like nobody's interested in you or like they just look through you.

Naomi describes what it was like for her. "I felt really alone when I came back to school after my car accident and three weeks in the hospital. A girl in my class said, 'Oh yeah, you haven't been here for a while, have you?' At that moment I realized that nobody in the class really cared about me. I felt like I could have died in that accident, and nothing would have changed. I was more alone at that moment than the entire time I was in the hospital."

Feeling alone is often about feeling that you aren't important to others, and that emptiness can make you miserable. But even if that feeling isn't based on reality (though it may seem real in the moment it's happening), it still makes life confusing.

your body

Part of being a teenager is dealing with a huge change in your physical appearance. You used to feel fine in the body you had as a kid, but now, when you look in the mirror, you don't recognize yourself. You're embarrassed about the new you. You think you're too tall, or too thin, or have too many freckles or not enough muscles. Maybe you hate your chest or your legs. The point is, when people don't like their bodies, they tend to avoid others so people won't look at them. They hang back, convinced that they're not attractive, and that people are going to make fun of them. They prefer to be on their own.

Right now your body is changing, and there's not a lot that can be done about that. Remind yourself that your body is what it is, with its imperfections and its good points. You can try to hide under baggy clothes, but that won't really solve anything. Instead, show off your best features—if you have nice arms, or strong calves, or great hair, focus on that. It's important to accept your body, and there's nothing stopping you from taking good care of it (through a healthy diet and exercise) and giving it every advantage (by dressing in a way that makes you feel happy with yourself).

It's really worth it to find ways to be comfortable with your appearance, because your attitude about your own body comes through in your

body language. It can change the way others see you. How? Here's an example. When certain super-cool people enter a room, everyone looks in their direction before they've even said anything. They give off a confident, secure vibe. What do they have that you don't? They feel comfortable with themselves, that's all. They're at ease, and it shows. If, on the other hand, you shuffle in awkwardly and are scared to speak, other kids will notice and be reluctant to hang out with you.

This situation can become a bad cycle. It starts off with you feeling bad about yourself, so you're not comfortable around other people. When they see the nervousness and anxiety in your body language, they're hesitant to approach you and start talking to you, which only makes you feel worse about yourself. So, if you want to make friends, start with yourself. Be confident. If you like yourself, other people will, too.

crush!

It's also impossible to have a healthy relationship without being secure mentally and physically. The body and feelings are tied together; when you worry too much, your body becomes tense and uncomfortable. If you aren't happy with yourself, it can affect your physical relationships.

It's also important to remember that it doesn't matter how experienced you are. Everyone goes at their own speed. If you haven't kissed a girl or boy yet, it may be because you need more time to feel physically and emotionally ready. Sure, dating is fun, but at age thirteen or fourteen

you're still very young—who cares if you haven't had a big, intense romantic relationship (or even a little, horrible one!). And you aren't a loser if you've only had dating nightmares! We all go through it.

"I've never been out with a boy; is that normal?" asks Naomi. "I think I must be gay," Greg worries. "Girls have no effect on me. I only find boys fun." Dominic wonders: "I masturbate a lot. Is that normal, and who can I talk to about it? I can't talk to my parents, so I feel like I can't talk to the doctor either." Another girl explains, "To fill the emptiness, I go out with lots of the guys I know. But they don't really care about me. We always break up, and it's very upsetting."

All these questions and others that teenagers ask are normal. It's really common to be confused about what you want in a physical relationship. When your body changes and hormones kick in, your desires change. Discovering exactly what you need and how you feel about kissing and all that other stuff is a gradual process. Not knowing what you want and where you fit in is frustrating and lonely, but you have to realize that now is the time for figuring that out. Everyone is going through the same thing. And you can try things step by step, at your own pace. Sometimes you do things without thinking, and then later look back on the experience to understand if the decision was a good or bad one. Sometimes you overthink. You still might not have all the answers, but just relax. Soon you'll work it out and hardly remember feeling so confused about all the details.

nobody
loves me!

When you're self-conscious, you aren't sure how to react to people, or how you measure up to others. Sometimes you feel like you're not loved, or that you're being rejected because you're not living up to what others expect of you. Your parents want you to listen to classical music, but you like hip-hop. They wish you were at the top of the class, but you're somewhere in the middle. It seems like they don't love you anymore, at least not the way they used to. It's the same with friends who don't understand your tastes. You like hiking in the woods, but all they want to do is wander around shopping malls. You can't communicate with anyone. At home, you and your parents have nothing to say to each other. You see each other, but you don't really *see* each other. At dinner you sit in front of the TV without any interesting discussion at all. The only conversation is boring and practical: "Pass the salt," "I need a new pair of soccer cleats," "Don't forget to buy more OJ at the grocery store . . . " and stuff like that. No wonder you feel confused and insecure.

Nicholas explains his problem. "I have two older brothers who are really athletic. My dad is that way, too. When I was younger, my dad and I would throw around a football or he'd take me to the batting cages. He even coached my Little League team for a few years. But then around the age of ten, I stopped being into sports. I really like computers and that became my hobby, and I decided not to go out for my school's sports teams. I know my dad was really disappointed that I didn't turn out to be the athlete he wanted, like my brothers. Since then, my relationship with him has disappeared, and he seems to avoid me. Although I have a big family, I feel alone because I'm not the same as they are. I have to deal with this problem all on my own. It's like my dad refuses to acknowledge me now."

Because Nicholas didn't meet his dad's expectations, he feels alone. He doesn't think his dad doesn't love him, he blames his dad for not loving him unconditionally—for not loving him for who he really is.

nobody
"gets" me!

People sometimes feel lonely without knowing why. Even though they have friends and family who care about them, they're still under the impression that nobody else understands them and that they're the only ones in the world who feel the way they do. If that describes you, no wonder you find it difficult to share your problems or discuss them with people! Although you might have lots of friends around you who think you're great, you can still feel horribly alone. People who seem like they have the most amazing lives can still feel sad and lonely sometimes. In the song "Lucky," from her second album, Britney Spears even sings about a star who cries all the time because she's so lonely. Even though she appears to have everything, there's still something missing. You would think a star should feel happy and loved, but everyone goes through times when they feel alone.

When you feel like this, it's like a void opening, a black hole. Sometimes you have deep thoughts and wonder endlessly about the meaning of life. Sometimes you feel like you don't know who you are. The loneliness you're experiencing is really more a sign of growing up than of actual isolation. Maybe you feel a little depressed, which is very common in adolescence; don't panic, it will get better. (And if it doesn't, there's nothing wrong with finding a therapist or school counselor to talk to.) If you talked about your feelings with somebody else your age, you'd probably find out that they're going through the same thing.

Maybe you're tempted to hide or block out the painful outside world. Or else you go to the opposite extreme and rebel or act out to attract the attention of your parents (or to punish them, because you feel they don't understand you). If you want to stop feeling disconnected from the world, you need to be sure of who you are first. Until then, it will be hard for you to relate to people.

are you
judging me?

If you are afraid that people who don't think exactly like you are judging you, you'll always be worried about their reactions. Do you freeze as soon as people look at you? Do you have the feeling they're sizing you up? It's perfectly normal to want to be accepted, especially at this stage in your life. Certain people's opinions are important to you, and that's understandable. But you shouldn't let other people's opinions or judgments of you dictate your behavior. Your relationships will be healthier if they aren't based on the fear of disappointing someone. Don't avoid people whose judgment you are scared of; most likely, they're just as worried about what you might think of them. And don't change who you are to make them like you. Remember, you're just as cool or smart or interesting as they are. Maybe they're just better than you at hiding what they don't like about themselves, that's all! The thing is, worrying about what other people think is silly; sometimes it takes a long time to learn you can't please everybody.

Your main problem is probably a lack of self-confidence. That's what Claire admits: "I think my loneliness is due to a lack of confidence in myself. I guess it comes from the way people treat me. If they're happy and want to hang out and talk to me, I can be happy and bubbly, too. But if they're standoffish, I feel very alone."

What Claire is admitting is that her behavior changes according to her friends' attitudes. She bases her mood on her friends' friendliness or lack thereof, so her confidence in herself is limited because it depends on other people. Claire feels undermined if they aren't friendly to her, even if she doesn't know why . . . even if they haven't actually criticized her or done anything wrong!

fear of disappointing
your parents

Lots of times, parents project their own desires onto children and it feels like a prison sentence for their kids. For example, lots of parents would like their children to get straight As. "You need good grades to get into a top college," they say. Yeah, but when you're trying hard but can't seem to do well in math (or science or whatever), what happens then?

One reaction might be to avoid contact with your parents, since they don't understand that you're either already doing your best or simply don't want to rack your brain and work like a crazy person. But avoiding your parents will only frustrate them and make things worse for you.

When you're searching to figure out who you are, nothing is more difficult than having someone tell you who you should or shouldn't be. It might seem easier, sometimes, to try and fit into the mold your parents have created for you. It feels good when you've pleased them and they praise you. And, of course, your parents want what's best for you. But if who you are inside doesn't match up with what they want you to be, trying to live up to their expectations can make you feel very alone. Why? Because your own desires haven't been respected, too. It's a tricky situation, which is why teenagers fight with their parents so much.

blending in

One way of avoiding rejection from other people is to try to be as much like them as possible. Then you won't seem weird to them; you might even impress them! When you feel alone, it's a natural tendency to act as if you belong to a particular group, by adopting their hairstyles, their clothes, their way of speaking, their mannerisms, their interests . . . as if being like members of that group will make lonesome

feelings go away. And sometimes it works, but it's only a temporary solution.

Having a group of friends is great, but being part of a group shouldn't make you lose sight of who you are and what really matters to you. It's easy for a crowd mentality to replace individual personality. Sometimes once you become part of a group, you feel you are "somebody." But this isn't always reality. The most important thing is to remain true to who you are. If you get to know yourself better, you'll be better at fighting feelings of being alone, whether you're in a crowd or not. You'll be able to face the world by yourself, which is a great feeling. Before you become part of a group, the questions you need to ask yourself are: Do I really want to hang out with this particular group of people? Do I agree with their way of looking at things? Or does it just feel safe to be with them? If you're hanging out with people you don't really like or admire, you might want to reconsider your place in the group.

It's pretty normal for teenagers to spend their lives in a crowd, or clique. Teens who'd rather keep to themselves or hang out in small groups of two or three are considered "loners." These teens feel different because their viewpoint isn't like everyone else's. Anna's whole class snubs her because she wears unusual clothes that she thinks are funky, but aren't considered trendy. So she goes and sits alone, trying to protect herself from the other students' weird stares. Anna's behavior just gives the other kids another reason to ignore her. Who wants to be friends with someone who isolates herself and seems so different?

Even if Anna basically liked being on her own, she'd eventually get fed up with other people telling her how to act or how to dress. The message she's getting is: you can't dress or act how you want to, otherwise, people will be mean to you and then avoid you because you're a loner.

If you're like Anna, you risk becoming the outcast, or the one kids want to avoid. You can't read alone in the schoolyard or sit by yourself

and think without other students giving you strange looks. You can't eat on your own in the cafeteria without surprised glances. And imagine what people would think if you went to the movies by yourself? At home, of course, you can escape your classmates' stares, but being alone at home isn't fun either, especially if you and your parents barely speak to each other. Or maybe your parents give you a rough time for spending too many hours alone in your bedroom. The point is, even if being alone seems easier, you can't go through life without interacting with others.

shyness

How much time you spend alone depends on your personality type. The shyest people are the most likely to find themselves alone. Of course, it isn't fair. But if you think about it, you can see why it happens. Basically, shyness comes from a lack of self-confidence. You're shy when you don't feel comfortable with others, when they're super-cool (at least in your mind) and you're scared of looking stupid. And the shyer you are, the more afraid you'll be to join a group or do anything to give people a reason to have opinions about you. So you keep to yourself.

Come on, don't be scared.

Ahhh, shyness . . . when your cheeks go bright red as soon as you open your mouth, when your knees wobble, when your hands get clammy. We've all experienced the symptoms. Unfortunately, now is the time when it's most intense. As you develop and get to know yourself better, you'll be more confident deep down inside, and you won't be so timid when dealing with people. These shy mannerisms will naturally fade as you grow older. Claire explains, "I think that I'm getting less and less shy. But when a teacher asks me to go to the blackboard, I still get sweaty palms and go all red. When someone I don't know very well speaks to me or asks me for something, I blush and can't talk. Many of my friends are like this, too, but some people are better than others at coping with it. I think being shy limits you, because sometimes you're too nervous to do certain things and you end up missing out."

ph1

Shyness doesn't cause loneliness or explain why you end up alone. It's just a result of being uncomfortable and unsure of yourself. You're shy because you want the love, respect, or affection of others but you're afraid you won't get it. In a sense, shyness is a type of aggression (non-violent, but aggression all the same), a reaction to someone who makes you afraid that they will reject you. You "fight back" by not sharing your real personality with them. Shyness also exposes the feeling of power-lessness that takes over you when you're faced with something new and difficult.

You don't talk much, huh?

Finding yourself alone in a class or group where everyone knows everyone else is never easy. It takes time to connect with people. First, you'll be seen as "the new boy/girl," but try not to be shy. It will help to be outgoing and friendly. Have faith that you will be accepted, and that others will eventually consider you as part of the group. Don't worry—they will!

turning
inward

Shyness can also make people turn inward. This means that social situations and being with other people can cause anxiety. Even though you may have dozens of people around you, you still feel completely isolated, caught up in a world that is alien to you. Sometimes when you feel like that, you revert inside yourself for protection.

A good example of this is the "iPod addict." As soon as they go out the door to school, they turn on their music and then crank the volume in

order to shut out street noises. In a way, they imprison themselves in the musical world they have chosen, whether it's Kanye West or Coldplay. An accident could occur in front of them, people screaming, arguing, etc., and they wouldn't hear or see anything. They're only in tune with their music, not with anything else going on.

So, what's the big deal? Listening to music is a good thing . . . as long as it doesn't cut you off from the world around you. Think about it: feeling lonesome is about feeling separate and different from the outside world. So, if you want to stop having that empty feeling inside, the best strategy is probably not to cut yourself off from what's going on outside.

when pride gets
in the way

Sometimes people are happy to be alone when they think that others aren't capable of understanding them. Maybe they don't want to interact because they aren't prepared to take a good, hard look at themselves. In a sense, it's easier to remain on your own and blame others than to get close to them and listen to their observations and criticisms, especially if some of what they say is justified.

Naomi found herself trapped in a situation that she couldn't get out of because she couldn't see how she might be to blame. She explains: "Ever since I was little, I've been a good student. And because I was smart, the other kids always kept their distance from me. Since I've been in high school it's gotten worse. They call me a 'brainiac'—as though that's the worst insult—and they think I don't have a life and just do schoolwork all the time. When I was a freshman, I was completely alone all year long; nobody came near me, except during the exams, when, all of a sudden, they came and said how smart I was and asked me to help them. So I convinced myself that they were idiots, and I said no. To me, it was a sort of protection, but the people in my class thought it meant I was too good for them. It took me a while to realize how stuck-up I had become. I didn't realize my brainy reputation might make me hard to approach. But I was just upset that the only time they talked to me was when they wanted help with schoolwork."

Naomi let her pride stand in the way of making new friends. What if

she had helped tutor the students who asked her for help (and we know asking for help isn't easy), and because of that, they would have gotten to know the real her? Maybe then they would have seen the kind, fun person she truly is. It's understandable why Naomi was skeptical of her classmates, but she could have used tutoring as an opportunity to change her social life.

narcissism

One type of loner is the "narcissist." Maybe you know the Greek myth of Narcissus, the handsome young man who was indifferent to all female advances. One day, he caught sight of his reflection in a pool and was so attracted to his own image that he couldn't stop looking at it. In the end he fell into the water and died.

Narcissus didn't love anybody; he remained alone because he was in love with only himself, and found contentment in looking at his reflection. Like Narcissus, when you're alone you aren't disturbed by the observations and criticisms of others. You're free to spend hours in front of the mirror admiring yourself and thinking you are perfect, while criticizing how flawed and terrible everyone else is (like your boring teacher, your controlling parents, and your annoying neighbor). And even better, when you're alone, nobody is going to contradict you! But is that any sort of solution? Definitely not. It stops you from moving forward; it keeps you from becoming integrated into the world you live in. The moral is, Narcissus died because no one can live without the friendship and love of others.

are you too
demanding?

Sometimes it's the desire for perfection that isolates people. You'd like to be perfect, and every time you make a mistake or find a fault in yourself, you beat yourself up over it, and then, of course, try to fix whatever you did wrong. Well, it's possible to go on improving and progressing all through life. But it's also possible that not only are you too hard on yourself, but also on other people, as well. Maybe you criticize others as soon as they do something you don't like or find hard to deal with. When people are very demanding of themselves, they also tend to be demanding of others. They have difficulty putting up with people and accepting them as they are, including even the small faults. Sometimes, because of this, demanding people would rather be alone than with friends or family. And when they do see others, they often spend the entire time criticizing them. If you tend to do this, don't be surprised if people don't want

to be around you—you have to remember that nobody is perfect and we're all dealing with our own faults and insecurities.

It's worth trying to see things and people in a more positive light or placing yourself in someone else's shoes. Be a little more forgiving of yourself, too. We all need to be cut some slack sometimes. Accepting others (and yourself) is a sign of strength and maturity, not weakness.

do you feel
rejected?

Although being alone can be more a state of mind than a reality, it is possible to feel alone because you really are alone, because you aren't accepted by the people you would like to get close to. At most schools, certain students end up being scapegoats and have to put up with all the aggression of a whole group. The reason for rejection can be physical—people can be jealous of how you look or just not like it! It's all too easy to find some detail that can be exploited in a person to single him or her out—you don't have to be out of the ordinary for that to happen! In fact, kids who aren't popular in their school might be the type who would be the most popular student in another city or country—or if they had lived in a different era. In the nineteenth century, for example, the most sought-after women were overweight by today's standards. Today, many feel pressured to be thin, but you only have to look at pictures of women like Marilyn Monroe to see how to show off curves!

The reasons for rejection aren't just physical. The highest achievers in the class (remember Naomi) can be subjected to mockery, perhaps because of envy. It's easier to make fun of someone you envy than to be like them. Being a member of a minority group is also a common reason for rejection. Maybe it's a student whose father works in a factory, while the other kids in the class have parents who work in fancy office jobs. Or the opposite: in a school in a tough neighborhood, a girl can get taunted or even beat up for being a "spoiled rich girl."

Once someone becomes a scapegoat, it can be very difficult for things to change. And students who think the teasing has gone too far and would actually like to be friends with the victim run the risk of becoming victims themselves, subject to the whole group's mean comments and actions. It takes guts to stand out alone in defense of someone who's being bullied.

You can also feel rejected by your own friends. You don't know why, but suddenly they don't want you around anymore. It can happen without warning—even if ten minutes later there doesn't seem to be a problem anymore. As Mandy says: "I almost never feel alone, except when my friends talk secretly and exclude me from the group, saying, 'Go away, we're not talking to you' or 'Mandy's listening—we'd better go somewhere else.' Then I feel alone."

Behavior like that is cruel. Obviously, when your friends turn on you, they're doing it to hurt you. And intentionally hurting someone is not being a good friend. At the same time, it's important to examine whether there are any underlying causes for your friends' behavior. There may be something unintentional and totally innocent on your part that some-times causes them to shut you out, or act out. If they are your true friends, then talk about it; ask them if you're doing something that bothers them or makes them uncomfortable. It's normal for friends to go through rough patches or need different things at different times. Just try to keep the communication lines open.

ph1

the need for
affection

When a relationship ends with a best friend or a group of friends, it can trigger a sense of emptiness, of something missing. When you're on your own, you can't laugh over the ups and downs with a pal. At a time when friendships are very important, falling out with a friend can seem like a disaster. Whether you stop being friends with the whole group or split up with your best friend, sometimes, literally overnight, the bottom falls out from your social life. The friends you used to be able to count on now seem to have declared war on you. Who can you count on now? And how are you going to handle being on your own every day?

Breaking up with a boyfriend or girlfriend can also seem disastrous. You were going out with somebody really fantastic, then things started to deteriorate, and suddenly one day it's over. Maybe you saw it coming, but that doesn't help the pain. Although friends try to cheer you up, it doesn't make things better. You feel abandoned and worthless and you wonder what you've done wrong. It's hard to think about anything except your misery. All of a sudden you feel totally insecure. Since your world seems to have fallen apart, you now have tons of questions about yourself.

You feel even more lonely because you're going out less. No more trips to the movies; no more seeing each other between classes. You're even more alone at home, too. You get fewer telephone calls; no more instant messages for hours; you no longer spend your evenings in blissful fantasies. At night you mope and complain about how unfair life is. Most of the time, parents aren't too helpful. Even when they are aware of the problem—which is not always the case—they tend to play it down: "You'll find someone else," "With time, things will seem better," "It wasn't that serious, was it?" They don't realize that, for you, everything's fallen apart. Not just the relationship you had with your ex, but everything you had built around it.

As a result you may let yourself slip into a kind of "Poor me!" state. You're gloomy, you don't want to talk about it, and you won't do anything to alleviate the pain. You say things like, "I'm never going to fall in love again; it hurts too much!" You have every right to your feelings, but sooner or later you're going to want to join in on life again, so try not to isolate yourself from the world.

losing someone
close

Sometimes, the physical absence of someone you love is much more difficult to endure. Like when somebody really close to you, a family member or a good friend, dies. Unfortunately, there are no miracle solutions for this kind of loneliness. But talk about it with people you trust. Don't block others out—that won't help. Step back if you need to gather your thoughts, but realize that isolating yourself will only make you feel sadder. If the grief is really too painful to bear, you should talk about it with a doctor or school counselor who could direct you to a specialist, like a psychologist or a therapist. There's no shame in asking for help when you need it. Also, time will help, even though it may not seem possible at the moment.

When you lose somebody you care about, you can feel alone in another sense, too. There's not just the empty place left by the loss of the loved one, but you can also feel lonely because your friends haven't been through what you have, and may not understand what you're dealing with. That's what Carol says: "I remember last year, as Father's Day approached, all my friends were wondering what they could get their dads. It was a very lonely time for me, because I didn't have my dad anymore, and I felt alone. I know I'm not on my own and I haven't been abandoned, but it still felt like that." On one hand there's the pain of the loss itself, and on the other, you feel different and separate from people who aren't experiencing the same kind of pain you are, even if they're trying to understand. It's like, now that you've lived through such a damaging event, you're in a new world with a new point of view. But try to allow those who love you to reach out to you. No matter how strong you are, you need support.

speak
up!

get organized!

HOW TO
STOP FEELING
LONELY

discover the arts

get in touch

keep a journal

making the
most of it

If you want to convince people that you're worth spending time with, start by convincing yourself! Don't get hung up on what you think is wrong with you. Obviously you can't make your hang-ups disappear instantly—it takes longer for that to happen. But it's doable. Maybe you think you're not intelligent enough,

One day I'll be a prince! You'll see!

or wish you could laugh at life more. People are always trying to change and make themselves better, and that's fine. But no matter what, remember that the change you want to make is to become a better version of yourself, not to be more like somebody else. We're all different; it's part of the beauty of being human. Wouldn't life be boring if we were all clones, and we all looked, thought, and spoke the same way?

The key is to transform your peculiarities into pluses. If you're really tall and people are always commenting on it, instead of hunching over so you'll look shorter, join the basketball team and carry your height with pride. If you're a bad dresser and don't know how to put an outfit together, ask a stylish friend for help the next time you go shopping. You could even ask to borrow some clothes from that friend. Maybe your hair is super-curly, and you wish it was smooth and straight. Why not flaunt it and wear it wild, or in an old-school 'fro, or even dread-locks? So you don't find it very easy to laugh or joke around? That's fine; just make the most of your serious side.

The fact is, if you manage to look at yourself in a more positive light, one that values you for who you are without constantly hoping to be per-fect, you'll be more relaxed and comfortable around other people. Of course, it's easier said than done, but start with small, everyday situations. Suppose, for example, that people at school make fun of the hat you just bought. If you think about it and can see why they think it's funny, laugh with them. But remember that if you really love the hat, no matter how silly it is, keep it and wear it and tell yourself what really matters is that you bought it because you thought it was special (like you)!

hiding beneath
your shell

One of the problems with feeling lonely is that if you feel isolated, you may start to take it out on people. You're scared of other people's reactions, and also scared of yourself. So, sometimes, it just seems easier to close yourself off and be unfriendly. If you've been rejected a bunch of times, it makes sense that you'd be frightened of another negative reaction. By being hostile and hiding beneath your shell, you're really just trying to protect yourself. It's a defense mechanism you've used when others have been mean and thoughtless. It's easier to feel like you're the victim of these bad people and to hide, rather than to consider that you may be part of the cause of your isolation.

Obviously, when you distance yourself, other people will sense your standoffish attitude, and they are going to be wary. This sets up a vicious cycle: you are guarded toward others, they notice this, they respond by acting guarded toward you. If this continues, it's impossible for any relationships to form.

Look at people who are immediately liked by everyone (or almost everyone). How do they behave? They're probably warm and friendly when they meet you and they make you feel like you're worth knowing. They may have never hung out with you before, but they talk to you like they think you've got something interesting to say or bring to the table. Which, by the way, is true! Or would be true, if you didn't hide behind a wall of shyness.

Do you think that people who are more open and friendly get hurt less often than you do? Probably not. It's just that they understand that friendly interaction is important, and that life is better without being constantly scared to put yourself out there.

speak up!

When you're lonely and feeling bad about it, say so. Don't suffer in silence. When people openly acknowledge that they are lonesome, they're halfway to accepting it and trying to get the better of it. It's helpful to be able to admit it—first to yourself and then to others. Analyze your behavior and feelings. Look around you, and decide what you like and what you dislike about yourself. Rather than constantly comparing yourself with others, try to understand what it is that makes you afraid to connect with them. Discuss it with someone you can trust, because talking about the problem can provide you with a fresh look at yourself or raise new questions that will help you move forward. It will get you out of the mental rut you've been stuck in, going over the same old questions and problems repeatedly.

If you feel lonely when you get home from school, maybe you could tell yours parents about it. They understand what it's like to feel alone. If they're usually at work during that time, they might be able to arrange for you to go to a friend's house or maybe they could come home a bit earlier a few evenings a week. No one deserves to suffer in silence. And there's no shame in saying that you're lonely and that it's getting you down.

and when things are
really bad

There is no better medicine for loneliness than having other people listen and pay attention to you. Why not go see your school guidance counselor; he or she is there to listen and help. You could also talk to a nice teacher, a nurse, or anyone you trust on the school staff. Above all, don't let feelings of depression get a hold on you without taking action. If you don't do anything, they could get worse.

What if the sad feelings have already taken over—then what? Let's say you're about to spend the weekend on your own with nothing planned, and dark thoughts are going around in your head? Pick up the phone and call a friend, a cousin, anyone you like and who can give you a bit of support. And if there isn't anybody able to do that, you can call a professional who is there to help you, or go online:

suicide: the Suicide Prevention Resource Center at
www.sprc.org, or call 1-800-273-TALK
abuse: www.break-the-cycle.org
health: www.kidshealth.org

The people who work at these helplines are trained listeners. They won't make fun of you or what you are feeling. And there are also many helpful articles you can read online.

If your feelings of depression won't go away, you may want to talk to a psychologist or therapist who will listen and help you to understand and get to the bottom of your problems. The first step toward getting better is recognizing that you can't do it alone and seeking out help.

get organized!

So, now you have a clearer idea of what causes you to feel lonesome, right? Well, it's time to try to reduce the amount of time you spend alone by getting together with people. When you know that you're going to have to spend a lot of time on your own, instead of complaining in advance, get organized! Having projects to work on will help you to manage the time and avoid boredom. And if you're successful in filling up some of the empty slots in your schedule, you're making progress!

What if you're dreading being by yourself over the weekend? Make a schedule of things you want to do. Feeling lonely late in the day? Ask an old friend to come over, or join an after-school club that you're interested in. Have you always wanted to take guitar lessons or learn karate? What about painting or crafts? You could even be a volunteer in your community. Of course, things aren't always that simple.

No one said it's easy to invite somebody over when you're worried about how they might react, or joining a group of people you're not familiar with.

But take some initiative, including that difficult first step. You have everything to gain. Even if you have to ask your parents for a ride somewhere, they'll probably be happy to help you out. Once you do it, you'll feel productive to be making the most of your days. But remember, it isn't enough to make plans; you need to put them into action. There's no point planning a fantastic weekend of activities and then collapsing in front of the TV, saying to yourself, "Actually, I can do all that next weekend" or "I can't believe I'm sitting here watching this lame TV show. I really have to get up," and then not moving a muscle!

too
organized

Be careful! Creating a full schedule doesn't mean you should hide behind an overload of activities.

This is Carmen's schedule: Monday evening, art lessons; Tuesday evening, Drama Club; Wednesday afternoon, school sports team; Thursday evening, Drama Club; Friday evening, incredibly, nothing! Sounds great. But it's not so great, as far as Carmen is concerned: "I'm not really used to being alone . . . I have so many activities, and when I get home, I do homework on the kitchen table because my bedroom is too noisy with my two younger sisters. I help my Mom get dinner ready and look after the younger kids. On the weekends we always have family around. The weeks fly by without me noticing. I really don't have time to get bored! All the same, I feel a bit empty inside. I feel different from other kids; I don't have the same lives as they do. I don't think about it all that much, but only because I don't have time to. Except sometimes, even though I'm surrounded by my family, friends, and activities, I feel lonely. My parents aren't on the same wavelength as me; they speak Spanish to each other and think that in America they can lead the same life as in Mexico. Basically, I think that I do so many activities to fill up that big empty space."

The sense of isolation that Carmen's describing isn't easy to detect; it's less obvious than the other examples we've mentioned. Why? Because excessive activity can sometimes mask feelings of loneliness. Because people can overdo things in order to hide an emptiness within. Emotional needs aren't necessarily satisfied by a bunch of activities.

What about you? Are you someone who always does too much and stays busy in order to avoid your feelings? Being constantly active is definitely a way to avoid dealing with the problem of feeling lonely. When you're busy, you don't have to think about it. But that doesn't solve anything either—you still have to deal with why you are feeling lonely.

get in
touch

If you're feeling lonely and can't find anyone to be friends with, you might be able to meet up with old pals or acquaintances. You may think you don't have any, but there probably are one or two. The girl from dance class three years ago who always made you laugh, or your best friend in elementary school, or the friend who moved last year, or the boy you swam with at summer camp.

If you're worried you'll annoy them by trying to get in touch, don't be. The opposite is usually true; old friends often love getting back in touch. After all, it's a chance for them to make friends and re-establish old links as well.

The easiest thing to do is to gather up your courage and write them a letter or send an e-mail. It's a lot less intimidating than having to think of things to say on the phone to avoid uncomfortable silences. This way your old pal has a choice of whether to reply or not. If you don't hear back, just give it time. Maybe they're too busy to write back or call at the moment. But more than likely, they'll get back to you soon, and be very excited to hear how you're doing.

You don't have much to lose, and you have a lot to gain. And even if you're not a great writer, just write them a line or two. A short note is better than nothing at all, especially if you really mean what you say.

plan
a party

It may seem complicated, but another good idea is to organize an event and include all the people you like. Throw a party, an evening at the bowling alley, a day at a miniature-golf course, a trip to the movies, or anything fun that you can do in your city or town. It's a smart way to get to know people and bring them together. Organizing plans also makes you organize yourself and motivates you to do something interesting with your free time.

If you feel really motivated, you could throw a party for your whole class. That way nobody feels left out because you didn't invite them! Otherwise, limit your plans to a few friends. If it goes well, you can always invite more people the next time. Or, for example, if you'd like to get better acquainted with other kids who like the same football (or basketball) team as you, why not invite them over to your house to watch a big game with you. It wouldn't need a lot of preparation, and you'd get to know them better.

Are your parents standing in the way of your party plans? Explain to them what's at stake: that you need to make friends with people in your class because you're having a hard time meeting people. They'll be much more likely to help you out once they realize how important it is to you. They want you to be happy, even if it disturbs their peace and quiet for one day! If you want to make things go even more smoothly with your

folks, write out a list of things you promise to do. For example, if you're having friends over, tell them you'll clean up afterward. They may even leave you and your friends alone to do your thing.

If possible, get a pal to help you organize. You'll have less to do, and will be less likely to forget something important, like music or food or games. It's also a way of establishing a closer connection with that friend, because you'll have planned everything together and had fun doing it. If you're inviting a large group, you might also want to ask some friends to help you make sure the celebration doesn't get out of control. But don't worry too much. The kids in your class will just be happy you threw a party where they had so much fun!

remember your
family

If you feel most alone inside your own family, you could try planning a meal. You could say, for example, "Tonight, let me handle everything. I'll do the shopping, cook the food, set the table, and wash the dishes! In return, you guys just have to be on time, turn off the TV, and promise not to argue."

The meal might help restore conversation, or you may finally be able to talk about something you've been dying to bring up but never found the right time, until now. It is an opportunity for you to show that you aren't a baby anymore: even if the meal is a bit overcooked, you did it from start to finish. Your parents will appreciate the effort.

You don't mind if it's a little burned, do you?

Another possibility would be to organize an outing. If, for example, your parents like museums or walks in the park, try to find a place that you'd enjoy visiting, too. Your parents will be glad that you took the initiative and made plans with them. It will be proof that you are capable of taking something on and seeing it through. It's time for your parent to see you more as an equal and less as a child.

get to know your
neighbors

Another way to stop spending time alone is to get to know the people who live near you. Nothing seems more intimidating than the kind of neighborhood where people keep to themselves. But even if you do live in a place like that, there have to be other young people around who are bored or lonely and wouldn't mind having a friend who lives nearby.

Once you find out if any kids live in your area, make the first move. You could start by holding a door open for them in your apartment building or waving at them if they're outside in the yard. You could be a bit more conversational, and say something like, "Hi. What school do you go to?" or "Where are you from?" If they seem friendly, you could suggest walking together some of the way in the morning to your respective bus stops or hanging out after school.

If you live in a small town, you probably know all the people your age. But there's nothing to stop you from getting to know them better. Maybe you already stand together at the same school-bus stop, but instead of standing silently in the morning as you wait for the bus, strike up a conversation, or, if that seems too hard, there might be opportunities to join into other conversations. The kids may be surprised at first, but you have to start talking to make new friends.

join a
club

Nothing is better at getting people out of a rut than taking on responsibilities, because they automatically bring you into direct contact with others. There are lots of possibilities to choose from. For one, you could become a class representative at school. But if having to put yourself up for election—and possible defeat—feels too stressful, there are other ways of being involved. School clubs are always looking for members who will volunteer to help run extracurricular activities. There are so many to choose from: photography clubs, creative writing groups, chess clubs, theater clubs, yearbook clubs, foreign language clubs, computer clubs, internet groups, choirs, bands, etc. All you need to do is find one that you're interested in and offer to do something!

School libraries sometimes ask for volunteers to shelve and cover books, and to help other students with the computers. Even if the job doesn't seem very exciting, it's a way to interact with people and have conversations where you don't have to think of a topic. If you're not super athletic, you can still be part of a sports team by becoming a team manager. Once again, you'll automatically have something to chat about.

Outside school, there are plenty of groups looking for members. There are groups for people who like to jog together, read together, or go camping. Sharing powerful group experiences with others enables strong links to be forged more easily.

If school is your strong suit, you might want to look into tutoring others. Or if there's a subject at school that you love—like math or physics—there's probably a club for that, too.

join a
sports team

It can't be said often enough: sports help people
see their bodies differently and accept them. They also help give you a
more positive attitude. And, of course, when you practice a sport, you
meet new people. "There's no talk during the practice. They need to
sweat individually," explains one football coach. Afterward, though,
there's a lot of laughter and a bond of togetherness.

There's no need to list all the possible sports here; you know
them already. But if you are a boy who's bad at football, or a girl
who hates ballet, don't assume that athletics aren't for
you. There are plenty of ways to get your body moving
that are just as beneficial, such as yoga, fencing, synchro-
nized swimming, diving, tai chi, climbing, walking, skating,
skateboarding, table-tennis, and many more.

It's best to decide right away what kind of sport
appeals to you: team or individual. The advantage
of team sports is that they quickly create a bond

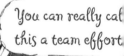

You can really cal
this a team effort

between people. Team partners and opponents become friends more easily than students in a class where there are fewer shared emotions. The experience of being in a classroom is more passive, and you aren't all working together toward a common goal. When you play a team sport, you all sweat together; you live through the same anxieties and make the same effort during the game, and the common experience you have is very powerful.

But if the team thing isn't your speed, you can always opt for an individual sport at first. That way, you'll focus all your effort on your own body's performance, and you'll get to know yourself better. Once you feel more at ease with yourself, you can try a team sport and make lots of new friends!

discover
the arts

This time it isn't about sweating together, but rather about creating together and/or on your own. It's a way of expressing yourself without having to talk much. Sometimes, when people are shy or have difficulty speaking, they get lots of support from a creative activity. It's as though the arts, or a craft, enable you to express what you feel without having to describe it in words. For example, you can vent your irritation, excitement, or anger through painting. It's an excellent way to channel your energy or aggression without taking it out on other people.

Oops! Maybe I got a little too carried away!

Take music for example. Of course, you can always play the violin all by yourself. But if you want some backup, it's better to join a conservatory or music academy. Don't be discouraged by the old-fashioned image of these types of places; these days they teach percussion, rock, and jazz, among other things. And there's the advantage of possibly playing in a band, group, or orchestra. Regardless of your level, you'll have the chance to rehearse with other musicians and participate in concerts, which is always a great experience no matter what instrument you choose. You'll be producing something and showing what you're capable of, plus you'll be doing it with other people! You'll be killing two birds with one stone: using the time you spend on your own to work on your instrument, and meeting people in the band or group you join. Plus, the friends you meet will share your love for music!

Let's not forget the theater. Lots of famous actors have said that they are actually loners when they're out of the spotlight. Being onstage is more comfortable because they're able to express themselves indirectly. When you play a character, you can forget your own personality and your problems. You become someone else for a little while, and for some people it's the perfect outlet. You also get to meet people and spend time rehearsing your lines together.

Another advantage of drama is that it teaches people how to relax and speak in public, which is always a useful skill. And it's an amazing feeling when, after months of preparation, you finally perform in front of an audience.

Artistic activities like these let you express yourself without entirely exposing yourself. You play at being someone else, which enables you to experience new emotions. But at the same time, you know it's only a

Beloved Juliet, wilt thou pass the salt?

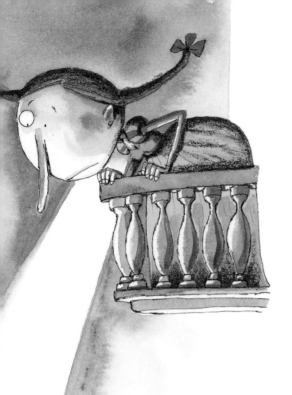

game: the risks are fewer. Best of all, you get the satisfaction of communicating your feelings and being creative!

Of course, there are also clubs for model-making, pottery, sculpture, drawing, knitting, quilting, creative writing, and a ton of activities that focus on artistic ability and commitment. Activities that develop manual skills can be a way of distracting yourself from your day-to-day problems while you focus on a task. All these possibilities provide a fresh way of looking at the world. And they also mean you become attached to new groups and meet new people, people who are going to have interests that are similar to yours.

keep a
journal

Another good way to understand yourself better and deal with the drama of daily life is to keep a journal. You don't need another person for that, just some quiet time, a pen, and a notebook. What counts is that you're honest with yourself; you should write down all your feelings, including the personal and painful things. If you get to know yourself better, you'll be more comfortable around others. Don't be afraid to be accusing, extreme, or cruel. Whatever your state of mind, try to record it as accurately as possible. Get it all out on paper, because it's a safe place. Then try to be objective; read what you wrote and analyze what happened and your reaction.

Lots of young people write in their private journals as if they're writing to an imaginary friend. Anne Frank, the Jewish girl who was forced to go into hiding from the Nazis, wrote to someone called Kitty. Her diary was like a daily letter where she was able to admit how upset or frustrated she was. Writing to an imaginary friend (who will understand perfectly because he can't answer back) can be an excellent way to give voice to your feelings and make loneliness easier to deal with. When you feel really alone, sometimes it's hard to communicate. When you write about what to do in certain situations and how the other person might respond, it will help you prepare to confront sticky situations in the real world.

SEEKING
SOLITUDE

solitude is necessary

FINDING SOLITUDE

the
real
you

accepting
solitude

take a closer
look

solitude is
normal

Despite all that's been said earlier in this book, it's important to be clear about one thing: being alone from time to time isn't the worst thing in the world. A few hours of calm during the day can be beneficial, especially if you want some time to think. Sometimes you need to be alone because it gives you space to make personal choices without being influenced by other people. Otherwise you might not be fully aware of what you're doing.

It's 100 percent normal to be alone. Think about it. You start life that way because you're born by yourself. Even twins, no matter how close they are to each other, are born one after the other and have to learn to breathe totally by themselves. Some of the greatest moments that you experience in life are felt

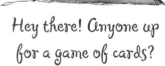

Hey there! Anyone up for a game of cards?

as an individual. Sure, you have friends and family who are proud of you, but the joy in your own accomplishments belongs to you alone.

When you think about it, you're the only person you'll spend your whole life with. Friends and loved ones will come and go (some will stay longer than others), but at the end of the day, you're all you've got. It's kind of scary, but also kind of exciting.

solitude is
necessary

Let's see what's inside.

A psychologist by the name of D. W. Winnicott describes three stages of aloneness: the fear of being alone, the desire to be alone, and the ability to be alone. What he means is that you have to experience being alone in order to be able to accept it. People sometimes find it hard to accept being alone, because it forces them to confront their own identity. It can be weird and uncomfortable, especially in adolescence, when you haven't really discovered yourself and don't know exactly who you are yet. This first stage of being alone can be really unpleasant, because you feel truly lonely. Then there's the second stage of being alone, where it becomes a refuge. At this stage when you're alone, you enjoy it because it means you don't have to deal with other people criticizing you, and you can have your own private thoughts without anyone interfering.

Lastly, there's the third stage, which is the ability or capacity to be alone. It comes when you find the boundaries and can achieve a happy medium between the necessary company of others and the space that solitude gives you for finding yourself and realizing your potential as a unique individual. Nobody can avoid being alone at least some of the time. It provides you the opportunity to dig down into the resources you contain and discover your creative gifts. Once you've realized that you are capable of enriching yourself and advancing, without necessarily being supported by other people, then you've taken a huge step forward.

You're probably wearing a questioning smile: "The resources I contain? What if I don't have any?" Of course you do! It's just that some people spend longer looking for theirs than others. But once you recognize your talents and special qualities, you'll find being alone a much easier experience.

I hope I find my personality soon.

Now, let's see. What personality shall I go for?

1st shy

2nd friendly

3rd aggressive

the
real you

Wait a second. Is it true that to be free you have to be alone? Well, actually—yes. To a certain extent, solitude is crucial for personality-building, gaining personal independence, and opening up to others. When you're with other people, discussing and sharing opinions, you're slightly affected by the nature of the group or the friend you're with. In most cases, you modify your personality to synchronize with whomever you may be around at the time. Different personalities tend to balance each other out. This is totally natural and perfectly normal—as long as you are aware of it.

ph3

You've probably noticed that you don't behave exactly the same way when you're with your family as you do when you're with your friends. You even act differently around certain friends. Depending on who you're with, you're more or less open, more or less funny, attentive, daring, etc. Everybody modifies his or her personality slightly, depending on the situation. It's okay, as long as you're not pretending to be someone you're not.

accepting
solitude

When you accept your own company, you're freeing yourself of the fear of other people. You're accepting that you don't need to be permanently under the control of a protecting group or dominant personality. When you accept your own solitude and don't immediately fight to escape it, you're ready to welcome others into your life without needing to put up protective, insulating barriers. You'll be more relaxed, because the relationship is no longer based on, "You *must* become my friend because I don't have any," but on its opposite, "Let's be ourselves and see if we can be friends."

Carol explains: "When I'm alone, I can question myself, see things (good or bad) in a different light, and rediscover my true personality, because, when I'm alone, I don't have to pretend. Being alone lets me

Aaaaaaaaagghh! This gang is suffocating me!

find myself again and have fresh ideas about people and the world. Solitude helps me grow up, develop, and remain objective when I make decisions."

Throughout your life, you won't be able to succeed in everything you do. Nobody can! Certain attempts and certain relationships will fail. Time alone helps people evaluate their setbacks, and, little by little, get over them. You can't expect other people to have all the answers for you; all they can give you is advice and some pointers. But the real solution will come from inside of you.

seeking
solitude

Although being alone can feel terrible at times, people also purposely think of solitude as a positive experience. Some of the people who read this book enjoy being alone! If you're like that, you already know that being alone doesn't have to feel like an enormous weight has been dropped on you! Solitude is also a freedom, a reward. People need to get to know themselves well, and solitude facilitates that. A short time of solitude can do you good and keep you grounded. Touching base with yourself from time to time is crucial. In fact, time spent examining

ourselves helps us recognize that we definitely need others, but that they cannot live our lives for us.

Another good reason to spend time alone is just so you can discover that being alone is enjoyable! If you head straight for your computer as soon as you get home, and spend hours on it playing games, e-mailing, or chatting, you're not necessarily trying to hide from the world. Maybe you just enjoy your computer! And that's fine, as long as you don't spend your entire life on it.

Some people like spending time alone because it gives them space to paint, write, play music, or develop some other talent. Others choose to veg out in their rooms, listening to music and philosophizing, while some

Stop, thief! He's stolen my precious moments of solitude!

enjoy reading for hours, stretched out on their beds. Finally, there are those who enjoy walking for hours by themselves, admiring nature, or running for miles and finding their physical limitations.

Remember, these moments of solitude are even more precious and important when they're interspersed with all kinds of activities. Being alone is most rewarding when balanced with a life full of friends and family. And it's even more pleasurable when it comes in the middle of a crazy, hectic day. Solitude reduces stress levels and helps you relax and unwind. It's almost as good as yoga!

take a
closer look

You can learn a lot from walking alone on the street, listening to the sounds of nature, catching bits of people's conversations, and seeing how others live. It makes you think about the relationships that form between people, and how they play out. Basically, a few moments of solitude can teach you a lot about life. It'll help you be more open to the world around you and to understand it better.

When you make up your mind to take time out to look around, you discover new things. You observe the personalities around you, and you witness the difference between how people appear on the outside and what they're like deep down. As you watch their development, you'll become more skilled at analyzing your own.

Have you noticed the different ways that other people act when they're lonely? How much attention do you pay to other people? Try to be a little more aware of the unhappiness or suffering that other people experience, and get closer to them. You could start by considering their emotions. Through small gestures of recog-

nition, like a sympathetic look or a pat on the back, you'll definitely cheer them up.

If your life is a routine, in which you do the same things, go to the same places, listen to the same music, and never go off your path, you're missing out on other ways of being and living. It's a small example, but let's say you love electronic music and it's all you ever listen to. But maybe if you listened to a friend's reggae CD, you'd be surprised how much it resonates with you and makes you feel. Open yourself up to the exciting world around you!

solitude to
create

While artistic activities can be one way to meet people, learn how to be less shy, and avoid loneliness, they can also be a way to accept aloneness and give it meaning. Painting, sculpture, music, and writing are all forms of creativity that demand thought and reflection before you can actually create something meaningful. The creative process requires the individual to mature and to reflect long and hard upon what he or she wants to show, produce, or express from within. Your work will reveal a lot about you, even if no words are used.

Certain artists throughout history have reveled in solitude as if it were the greatest victory—the most complete form that freedom could take! It was a way of living apart from a world that did not understand them. They sought solitude and they appreciated it. The famous poet Emily Dickinson was known for living a life of solitude; in fact, some think her poetic genius is the result of her spending her life alone. (Of course, she was also considered a hermit by some!) But no matter what, before you reach that kind of desire for creative solitude, you need to experience what it means to be open to others!

adulthood vs.
solitude

Once you reach adulthood, being alone becomes a different situation. Sometimes it is a luxury. Adult relationships focus more on cooperation in work and life, and less on emotional needs and problems. Adults all have responsibilities that require them to work together, like running businesses or running a household. Grown-ups still have feelings and needs, obviously, but they have busy and demanding lives that take up a lot of their energy. As an adolescent, your life consists mostly of going to school, where you absorb information, which is a more passive experience. You have more time for emotional relationships and for questioning existence.

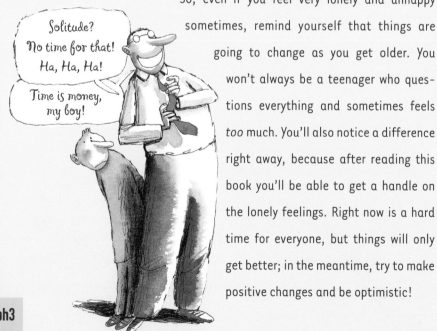

Solitude? No time for that! Ha, Ha, Ha!

Time is money, my boy!

So, even if you feel very lonely and unhappy sometimes, remind yourself that things are going to change as you get older. You won't always be a teenager who questions everything and sometimes feels *too* much. You'll also notice a difference right away, because after reading this book you'll be able to get a handle on the lonely feelings. Right now is a hard time for everyone, but things will only get better; in the meantime, try to make positive changes and be optimistic!

an exercise

In order to take a closer look, it's important to try to understand what causes your loneliness and where it comes from. Is it your attitude or your nature that makes things the way they are? Here are some questions that can help you figure it out. Choose a moment when you are feeling good and have some time to sit quietly, take a pen and paper, and try to respond to the questions below as honestly as possible. This isn't a graded exam; there are no right or wrong answers . . . Your answers are solely for the purpose of getting to know yourself better!

• In what kinds of situations do you feel alone?

• Do you have the opportunity to minimize the number of these situations?

• When someone suggests an activity to you, do you always refuse? If so, why?

• When you do participate in activities, either alone or in a group, do you find it satisfying?

• Do you take part in extracurricular activities?

• If you were to change some aspect of your attitude, do you think it would help you make friends or relate to others?

• Do you give the impression of being aggressive toward others? What is it about them that tends to aggravate you?

• Do you find that your personality changes when someone is with you? In what way?

• Do you believe that your shyness is the underlying reason for your loneliness?

• In your class or in your circle of friends, is there anyone you would like to get to know better? Try to think of five concrete ways you could achieve this goal.

• What do you think would help you gain more confidence in yourself?

And now? Have you taken the time to respond to these questions? Keep them in the back of your mind, and the next time you're feeling alone, force yourself to think of more ways to respond. Remember, everyone is trying to find themselves—so enjoy the journey of getting to know you!

suggestions for further reading

Books

The Burn Journals
By Brent Runyon (fiction)
(Vintage, 2005)

The Perks of Being a Wallflower
By Stephen Chbosky (fiction)
(MTV, 1999)

Loser
By Jerry Spinelli (fiction)
(HarperTrophy, 2003)

Jonathan Livingston Seagull
By Richard Bach (fiction)
(Scribner, 2006 [1970])

Be True to Yourself: A Daily Guide for Teenage Girls
By Amanda Ford (nonfiction)
(Conari, 2000)

On Love and Loneliness
By Jiddu Krishnamurti (nonfiction)
(HarperSanFrancisco, 1994)

Web sites

Suicide: www.sprc.org (Suicide Prevention Resource Center)
Abuse: www.break-the-cycle.org
Health/depression/general: www.kidshealth.org
General: www.girlsandboystown.org

index

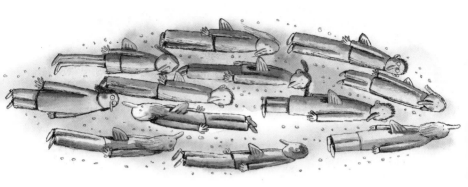

about the authors

Pascale Perrier became a librarian at a school in the Paris area after completing her literature studies. A member of a French guild for children's book authors and illustrators, she organizes writing workshops in schools. As an author, she tackles issues important to children and young adults with straightforwardness and humor.

Erin Zimring is an editor at *TEEN Magazine* and the author of many advice columns and articles. She lives in Los Angeles, California.